CONTAINER GARDENING:

A BEGINNER'S GUIDE TO GROWING PLANTS WITHOUT A BACKYARD USING CONTAINERS. COMPANION PLANTING AND VERTICAL GARDENING. THE ULTIMATE GUIDE ON VEGETABLES AND FRUITS CULTIVATION

WRITTEN BY:
SAM WILLIAM GROSS

Table of Contents

Introduction

Gardening has always been a basic activity of mankind. However, in the past people did this because they needed to survive – they planted food, basically. In the recent years though, gardening has become very much popular even in the urban setting, where agricultural pursuits are normally not easy to follow because the space in the city is limited for most of the people out there. What is it that makes so many people be attracted towards gardening in the city, especially when this is not something, they do for survival any longer? Even more, what is it that makes container gardening more popular in the urban areas than other types of gardening are? Even more than that, container gardening is a long-term investment no matter how you look at it. You may invest in pots and maybe even in sub-irrigated planters now, but for many years from now on, the only things you will have to invest in will be the plant seeds – nothing more.

Gardening has become more popular with many people and everyone seems to be looking into creative and space-effective ways to do this. In this guidebook, we will be exploring a number of topics that revolve around the art of gardening and how it can be done in containers. If you don't have much space (maybe because you live in an apartment), this could be a very good option for you.

Since container gardening makes the gardening process simpler, don't be surprised that your children love it. Bearing this in mind, container gardening can be a perfect way of bonding as a family. While you get to enjoy the quality time and share knowledge, your kids also enjoy healthy veggies and growing success.

You need lots of water when you water a garden as a whole. Whether you are working with a shortage of water supplies, or you are preserving water for other domestic uses, gardening with container is an excellent choice.

If your yard has a lot of shady areas that make growing a traditional garden difficult, you will enjoy container gardening as you have the liberty of moving your garden around as necessary to meet the sun. If lack of sunlight was your issue with gardening, container gardening has given you a new option.

Container gardens can be easily moved around. This makes it difficult for diseases and pests to survive, which amount to your garden's safety. You would be spending lesser amount of time combating pests trying to destroy your garden. Thus, you enjoy gardening more.

Container gardening makes gardening much easier by creating more suitable atmosphere for plants to strive with fewer pests than a large garden. Consequently, it produces healthier plants.

As you can see, there is quite a lot to learn about container gardening, but we guarantee you that it will be worth it. You will have a nice and constructive activity to hang on to together with your family, you will be able to use fresh herbs right from your very own garden and you will be able to relax in a great way!

Lastly, gardening in containers is convenient in term of planting, caring for your plants and harvesting your bounty.

Chapter 1. Advantages of Growing Plants in Containers

The Benefits of Container Gardening

There are various reasons why a lot of people start their own container garden. They are easy to manage, and they are very convenient. You can always bring them with you, especially if you frequently move, they can serve as accents to the different rooms in your house, they are space-efficient, and they are very cost-effective. Here are some more of the benefits that container gardening has to offer.

- **Soil can be adjusted according to plants' requirements.** If you live in a place where the quality of soil is poor, it might be impossible to successfully grow and harvest plants, but with container gardening, you can easily buy soil or create a soil mix that your plant will fruitfully grow in. In addition, if the plants you wish to plant have different soil requirements, then you can simply place them in different containers and fill the containers with the correct soil types.

- **Weeding will be much easier.** Because your plants are enclosed and contained in containers, weeding will be much easier and not much work.

- **Confines wild-growing plants.** When wild-growing plants are freely planted in a garden, they can sometimes cause problems, as they tend to overtake other plants and grow in different places. With container gardening, however, this is not a problem, as the containers are able to enclose and contain the plant. If the plants grow too big for their containers, you can decide to transfer the plants and submerge them in your garden without removing them from their containers.

- **Protects plants from wild animals.** If there are wild animals in the place where you live, plants planted in your garden might get destroyed or eaten. To avoid this, you can start an indoor garden instead.

- **Watering will be easier.** Different plants have different water requirements. If you plant to grow various plants, watering will be much easier because you can simply water them individually without the hassle.

- **Bringing them with you is easy.** If you frequently move to a new house or travel, container gardening is very ideal. Since they are in containers, you can effortlessly bring them with you without putting pressure on them and without stressing them out.

- **Moving them around will be effortless.** Just like water requirements, different plants have different sunlight requirements too. One of the best things about growing plants in container gardens is that you can easily move them around your house to make sure that they get the right amount of sunlight that they need. If it's winter season, you can follow the sun and place them in an area where the sun shines best, or if it's summer season and the sun get too hot, you can relocate them to a place where there is partial shade.

The Disadvantages of Container Gardening

There are a limited number of disadvantages to container gardening. Some of them are as follows:

- **Limited space.** Since plants are in a confined container, their growing space is confined as well.

- **Better for small plants.** Container gardening is ideal for small plants. Usually, plants which are commonly grown out of containers, are edible ones like herbs.

- **Frequent watering.** Although watering will be much easier if you have a container garden, you will find yourself watering more often. The reason is because the soil, as well as the moisture, are restricted to the dimensions of your containers.

- **Frequent fertilizing.** Frequent watering can wash away the plants' essential nutrients from the soil. Therefore, you might need to fertilize more often than you normally would if they were planted in the ground.

How to Get Started on Container Gardening

Container gardening is a growing trend that gives people easy access to vegetables, herbs and some fruits. It allows anyone, even those with just a limited amount of space, to grow, harvest and use their own plants. Listed below are some guidelines to help you get started on container gardening.

- **Containers.** The most important things you have to consider when choosing containers are your budget, what type of plants you want to grow and where you will grow them. If you are going to grow shallow root crops like onions, you will only need small containers that are about 6-10 inches in size. If you want to add succulent vegetables which need more root space, you will have to invest in 5-gallon containers. Plastic containers are the cheapest ones available. There are also containers made out of wood, but it is best to avoid them, as they might be treated with chemicals, which may eventually leak and get into your plants and eventually into your food. Ceramic containers are the best containers to use, although they are also the most expensive. Whatever material you choose, though, just make sure that they have suitable drainage.

- **Soil.** Soil needs to be healthy, moist and properly drained for plants to grow healthy. Make sure that the soil meets the requirements of the plants.

- **Space.** The kind and number of plants you can grow will also depend on how much space you have. Before you go out and purchase your containers, make sure that you have extensively studied the areas where you can place them. For example, if you do not have enough space on your deck or windowsill, you can decide to use hanging baskets. If your house does not get enough sunlight, then you might want to grow plants which are more shade tolerant.

- **Planting.** Once you got the containers, soil and space planned out, you can now purchase the seeds. But before planting them, you will need to germinate them first. All you must do is pour your soil mixture into a baking tray and water it. Make sure that the soil is thoroughly wet and place the seeds 2 inches apart from each other, under ¼ inch of soil. Place the baking tray in the area where the sun shines the most and water them every day. In a few weeks, you should see short shoots, and once they have leaves, gently remove them from the baking tray and transplant them about 3 inches down the soil in your chosen containers. Read the packaging to determine how far apart from one another they should be placed.

Planning Your Container Garden

Nothing beats the feeling of getting to use your own herbs and vegetables, and even flowers, straight from your own garden. There is a wide variety of plants that can be planted and grown in a container garden. With the right amount of planning, you can easily grow just about any type of plant you choose, given that their living conditions are met, of course.

- **Plan which plants to grow.** Plants have certain requirements that need to be met in order for them to grow properly. Therefore, you cannot just plant whichever plant you desire. You have to take into consideration the weather, climate and overall environment of where you live. Make a list of plants you want to grow and check their sun, water and soil requirements.

- **Evaluate your house.** Before you buy seeds or seedlings, carefully evaluate your house. Determine the areas which get the most sunlight, count how many hours the sunlight shines on those areas and identify the places which are partially shaded. Once you have listed those down, compare the requirements of the plants that you wish to grow and choose accordingly.

- **Determine where to place the plants.** If the area in your house which gets the most sun does not have enough space, choose to hang your containers or create shelves to place your plants on. You can also choose to place your plants somewhere else and then move them outside to get some sunlight; however, the constant moving may stress them out, which can hinder their growth.

Essential Supplies

There are many tools and supplies that a gardener could use; however, there are only 7 essential supplies that every container gardener should have. These supplies are important to have, as they help make sure that you properly maintain your garden and keep your plants healthy and beautiful. Taking care of a container garden is much easier than a huge garden

- **Gardening gloves.** Some people can do without gloves, especially when they are only tending to a container garden. However, to those people who squirm at the sight of dirt, soil and insects, gloves can be of really big help. Aside from that, though, gloves can provide your hands with protection, especially when you are tending to plants which have thorns and when you are handling sharp tools.

- **Watering can.** All gardeners should have a watering can. However, buying a new one is not a requirement. If you have old jugs of juice, water or milk, lying around, you can rinse them thoroughly and use them to water your plants. The only advantage of having a real watering can is that the water is dispersed, making it fall like rain, which makes it gentler for the plants. If you decide to use your old jugs instead, just make sure that you cover them and pierce some holes on their covers. This will avoid hitting your plants hard with water and prevent having excess water which can result in your plants having fungus and other related diseases.

- **Trowel.** A trowel is an important garden tool that can be used to loosen up soil and rake through compacted dirt. You can use your hands if you do not care about getting your hands dirty but using a trowel will do the job faster and easier. Plus, it will also protect your hands.

- **Pruners.** Never ever use scissors in place of pruners. Some people rely on their scissors to cut off dead foliage from plants. Although scissors can do the job, they are not ideal to use because they are not as sharp as pruners. Using scissors will not give your plants a clean cut, especially if used on thicker plants, which can cause serious infections and diseases. Aside from that, plants will leave some sticky residue on your scissors that will make them rust, which eventually will make them useless.

- **Organic pesticide.** If you are okay with touching, handling and removing insects and worms from your plants, it is fine not to make use of an organic pesticide. But, if touching various insects makes you shudder, you can choose to use an organic pesticide to protect your herbs. Before you buy an organic pesticide, though, make sure that you read the labels and instructions, as some pesticides are specifically made only for certain plants. In addition, if the plants you need to use some pesticide on are edible, it is best to not directly spray the pesticide on the plants, even if it is made out of organic materials. What you could do is remove the insect from the plant and spray the pesticide on the insect. This will make sure that your plants, and eventually your food, are organic and free from any chemicals.

- **Strings and sticks.** Some plants, even if grown out of containers, may still need support in order for them to grow. Strings and sticks are necessary tools, especially for those who want to grow plants that need some support straightening up. It is easy to find strings and sticks in gardening stores. They are usually available in various designs and colors, so you could match them with the colors of your plants or make them blend in, so they are not too obvious and do not draw the attention away from your plants.

- **Fertilizers.** Even if your plants are doing fine without fertilizers, it is important to keep some in your home. Just like pesticides, some fertilizers are made specifically for certain plants; therefore, you need to check what types of plants you have, so you can buy the appropriate fertilizers for them.

Chapter 2. Container Garden Design

The concept of container gardening is simple, but there is more to growing plants in container than merely putting together a collection of plants. It takes a bit of creativity to have a garden that compels compliments from admirers. Your garden is not really a garden until it is well organized and well arranged, such that it gives an attractive look and a refreshing feel. Below are design tips you can consider and work with to create a beautiful container garden of your choice.

1. Your Choice of Container

The first thing to consider when designing your garden is your choice of container. The container you choose is one of the factors that determine how appealing your garden will be. These are the common types of containers and what you may need to know about them:

Terra Cotta: it is known to be non-resistant to frost, they are usually heavy, but a variety of them can make your garden visually appealing. They are not too expensive and keep in mind that unglazed terra cotta has good air circulation.

Wooden Containers: When you use wooden containers for your garden, their natural look gives your garden a refreshing holistic and earthy feeling. Proper maintenance is, however, needed to prevent the wooden containers from degrading. A recommended course of action is to line them with burlap or plastic and use low chemical sealers to avoid deterioration and damage to plants. After applying the sealer, ensure to wait for about a day before transferring your plants into the container.

Plastic Containers: These types of containers are lightweight, unlike terra cotta, and are sold in different varieties. Although they do not readily allow much air circulation, they can, however, be made to look like clay or other materials to give your garden a visual appeal.

Moss Containers: Containers like this enables you to grow plants through the sides and not only through the top. They are mostly used in hanging baskets.

Metallic Containers: These types of containers absorb heat readily and are recommended to be used only for heat-tolerant plants.

Other containers used by gardeners are milk jugs, bushel baskets, planter boxes, etc. It is important to use containers that can conveniently accommodate the root of the plant you want to grow and also give your garden the visual display you desire.

2. Choice of Color

When designing your garden, the thing you consider is the color scheme you choose. You could try out a monochromatic color scheme, analogous colors or complementary colors depending on the color of the container you chose.

Analogous Colors: Analogous colors are colors, usually a group of three colors that are close to one another on the color wheel. An example is a group of blue, blue-violet, and violet. Keep in mind that cool colors like blue are best fit for colored containers like terra cotta, and warm colors like yellow or red will go best with wood containers or, in some cases, terra cotta.

Complementary Colors: Complementary colors are simple colors that are contrary to each other on the color wheel. They are any two colors where one is the direct opposite of the other. Examples include a shade of blue and orange color scheme, red and green, yellow and purple, etc.

Monochromatic colors: Monochromatic color theme refers to different shades of a color. When you choose a monochromatic color, it gives an attractive look when a contrasting container is used to compliment it. An example of a monochromatic theme is a theme of purple shades – indigo, deep purple, lilac, and lavender.

Explore: You may as well creatively explore your choice of color for your garden. Go ahead and try out any combination of colors you want but ensure that it gives your garden an alluring effect.

3. Your Plants Arrangement

Plants arrangement is critical when you are designing your container garden. Usually, two ways of arranging plants within a container are according to their habit and according to their size.

According to habit: The terms used for plant habits are filler, thriller, and spiller. These three can be combined in a single container. While fillers refer to plants with mounding ability, thrillers refer to upright plants, and spillers refer to trailing plants.

According to size: Arrange your garden by grouping your plants according to their height. Arrange them in such a way that you have tall plants growing at the back and the small plants growing in front. Ensure that the groups of plant sizes you are putting together all complement one another.

Explore: You could as well explore and get creative with your plants. Try out plants with a variety of textures as spillers and fillers to make your garden design less stilted. You could also arrange your garden according to a similar pattern or function— for instance, herbs that grow well together, flowers with complementing petal colors, etc. Don't be afraid of exploring your creativity. You never can tell how beautiful the result of your ideas will be.

4. Location

The last thing to consider in ensuring a perfect design for your container garden is the location of your garden. As earlier said, your garden is not really a garden until it is well organized. You could turn anywhere and anyplace to your garden; the key is in the arrangement and organization.

Hanging Planters: If you are to use hanging planters, ensure that the background from where the baskets are hanging allows the plants' colors to radiate well. As a recommendation, using a white backdrop will help in achieving this alluring effect when the blooms from the several well-arranged hanging baskets start popping out.

Containers on the tabletop: You can utilize your outdoor furniture and place your containers on them. If they are well arranged and organized, they can give your backyard a brilliant attraction and a refreshing feel.

Depending on where you choose to create your garden, try to be creative with the arrangement. Utilize your doorsteps and stairs to create different levels of height and a general visual appeal for your garden.

Chapter 3. Which Plants Do Well in Containers

Medicinal Herbs

There are several different types of herbs under the medicinal category, all of which can go into containers, but the soil and watering temperaments will be different. Let's take a look at them in their categories.

Wet Soil

Containers can be constructed, and the soil can be mixed in order to make a suitable home for a plant that loves water by using clay and peat in the mix to increase its water retention. You also want to use larger pots and not clay because smaller pots and clay pots will dry out a lot quicker. Herbs that love wet soil in containers includes:

- Gotu Kola

- Calamus

- Skullcap

- Yerba Mansa

- Boneset

- Vervain

- Meadowsweet

- Yellowroot

- Nettles

All of these herbs are used for medicinal purposes.

Well-Draining Soil

Try adding pine bark or coarse sand to your soil to increase its drainage. Perlite is also a good option. You should only water these herbs when the soil has dried out. If you're in a climate that has a lot of humidity, you might want to put them in an area that's far from the rain. Be careful to water only the soil and not the foliage because these herbs are more susceptible to fungal diseases. These herbs include:

- Ma Huang

- Prickly Pear

- Rosemary

- Lemon Verbena

- Garden Sage

- White Sage

Shade or Partial-Shade Herb Plants

If you want to grow "cold-weather" plants in a hot climate, then you should provide them with an afternoon shade to keep the plant happy.

These plants include:

- Jiaogulan

- Wild Geranium

- Black Cohosh

- Blue Cohosh

- Goldenseal

Sensitive Herbs

Herbs that are sensitive to the cold months and that should be brought indoors are in this category. Many of these plants can be overwintered in a basement or attic because they will go dormant over the winter.

- White Sage

- Lemongrass

- Ginger

- Turmeric

- Bay Laurel

- Aloe Vera

- Citrus

Ornamental

Most herbs can also be used ornamentally if you'd like, but there are some that have very beautiful flowers, an enticing aroma, and a deep green or unique foliage that adds a bit of flare to a container herb garden. Take a look at some of these ornamental herbs you could use to spice things up!

Silver Thyme

Silver thyme will get about twelve inches tall and has a lavender to pink blossom in the summer months. It's an evergreen that will need a twelve-inch-wide by twelve-inch deep pot in order to flourish. The fragrant, silver leaves makes a bushy texture in the garden. It loves sunny locations and prefers a sandier soil. It's also an excellent addition to tea and sauces if you feel inclined to harvest it.

Oregano Blooms

Origanum leavigatum has a purple to pink blossom that blooms for a long time. It grows to about two feet tall and has dark green leaves with a purple tint. Unfortunately, these herbs are not very good for cooking, but they do have a beautiful scent and a nice appearance. Herrenhausen has masses of pink flowers that have maroon bracts on the purple stems while Hopleys is a taller plant with long-blooming, deep pink stems.

Roman Chamomile

Chamaemelum nobile is a one-foot tall plant with white blossoms that bloom all summer long. It's extremely aromatic with an apple to pineapple scent. The threadlike leaves can also be used in teas; the young leaves are the one you want to use for your tea. In the summer, the blossoms are white with an almost daisy-like appearance. This herb loves moist, rich soil and will grow to a foot tall in a proper pot.

Berggarten Sage

Also known as Salvia, this two-foot-tall plant blooms in the early summer and has violet to blue flowers. The foliage is compact, shapely leaves that are dark green in color. At two feet tall, it's perfect as a backdrop for shorter container plants in the front. The dusty green leaves are a beautiful background for almost any container garden. You can also use the leaves medicinally as a tea in order to treat throat and lung problems. This sage can also be used to flavor meats and potatoes.

Catmint

Nepeta X Faassenii is a herb that cats adore and is also known as catnip in many regions of the globe. It's an eighteen-inch tall, bushy plant when it's in the right conditions, and has lavender blossoms that will bloom all through the summer. It also attracts many beneficial insects to the garden with its blooms, so while it's not normally edible for people, it can be used in container gardens to attract bees and other small insects to pollinate vegetables.

Catmint light green foliage and should be cut back throughout the season to encourage it to bush out and blossom more.

Salem Rosemary

Romarinus officinalis 'Salem' makes a beautiful, two-foot long backdrop for many other plants that bloom. The blossoms on this herb are a nice blue color and it's an early bloomer in the spring, so it provides color where many herbs are not yet able to bloom. It's an evergreen that has green, shiny needle leaves that weave through the container like thread. You can prune it down to the level you'd like throughout the growing season and use the pieces you harvest in soups and stews after you've dried them.

This plant likes fertile soil, a lot of drainage, and plenty of sunlight.

Cardoon

Cardoon has a purple blossom that makes itself known in the mid-summer and grows to around five feet tall. Therefore, it's best planted on its own in a large pot to keep it happy. It has gray-green leaves that arch and frame in order to showcase the purple thistle-like flowers. This herb is also edible. The stalks and leaves can be blanched and consumed, as well as the unopened flower heads.

This plant prefers a sunny, well-drained area.

Sweet Cicely

Myrrhis odorata is a late spring bloomer with white flowers that grows around two to four feet tall. This is a shade tolerant herb that has a fernlike appearance that grows in a mound with bright-green leaves. In the late spring, it's topped with a white star-shaped flower that has a shiny brown seed when it's finished. It does the best in partial to full shade in moist, rich soil.

The seeds and leaves have a sweet anise flavor that goes well with desserts, especially those made with fruits.

Anise Hyssop

This plant has a bright red bloom that appears in the late summer. The plant grows to about two to six feet tall, depending on the container it's placed in and has gray-green leaves. This plant prefers a well-drained, sunny area.

The flowers have an appealing taste, like a sweet anise, and it's delicious in salads. This is also another plant that's excellent for attracting bees and other beneficial insects to the garden.

Garlic Chives

Allium tuberosum have a white bloom that appears in the late summer. The plant grows to eighteen inches tall and prefers a sunny location with sandy, fertile soil. It also blends in well with its neighbors, like a flowering tobacco plant or some coneflowers. It has starry white flowers that catch the eye easily. After the flowers bloom, it's best to cut any of the seeds heads off and use them for decorative purposes because the seeds are vigorous growers. The flat, garlic-flavored leaves can be picked throughout the growing season in order to add to sauces, soups, and dips.

Now that you know the best herbs for different purposes in your container garden, let's look at the easiest ones to grow!

Best Herbs to Grow for the Beginners

In this topic, I'll tell you more about how to grow these herbs so that they thrive during the growing season. I'll also let you know if you want to plant certain ones alone or together with other herbs to make an attractive arrangement.

Mint

Mint is a really versatile container crop that can be used in chutney, mojitos, and many desserts. It's so easy to grow because it will cope with anything from a shady spot to a full sun location and still produce nicely.

However, mint is known to be a little greedy because it needs regular fertilization in order to grow well. You want to put each plant in a three to four-gallon container and keep the soil moist in order to be sure it grows to its full potential. You also want to pick the leaves regularly to keep it from slowing down. It'll easily grow into a bushy, large plant that will yield a constant supply of leaves all through the growing season. Once the plant has been established, take out of the container every spring after the winter dies back and divide it into halves so that you can either give plants away or make your collection larger.

There are numerous varieties of mint, and all of them are excellent for growing in containers. Some are more suited for tea while others are best for cooking.

Chives

Chives are an excellent herb for beginners because they are so easy to grow, and they are versatile when it comes to their uses. You can snip a little off for a salad, some more for soup, or just add it as a garnish to almost any dish. The flowers are really sunny in the spring and taste delicious, and bees adore these plants. This is another that is very easy to grow because it'll only need four to five hours of sunlight. Just be sure they don't dry out because they like damp soil!

Sage, Bay, Thyme, and Rosemary

These are all classic herbs that can be grown in container gardens. They're unique with their flavor and are often combined in order to make a stock, stew, a meat dish, or a pasta dish. They do not like wet roots, so you want well-drained soil and don't over-water them. You can grow the sage from seed, but the others should be grown from cuttings because the seeds tend to crossbreed.

Parsley

Parsley is very slow to get started from seed, so don't be upset if it doesn't start pushing through the soil for four to six weeks! Once it's established, though, it'll provide leaves for two years before the parsley will flower and die. Just remember to keep the roots damp but not wet and fertilize it if you start to see yellow leaves.

Coriander

Coriander will quickly flower and go to seed if it's planted in the spring. You can attempt to delay this by keeping the plant well-watered, fertilized, and grown in a shady area. If you cut the leaves regularly, the plant will last longer. Eventually, the plant will flower anyway and die. The flowers are perfect for salads and the seeds are delicious, so don't be too upset when it does flower.

It's better to sow the seeds during a hot time of year, like August in the northern states, that way the plant will last longer.

Basil

Basil loves the warmth and is best grown in a bright, warm sheltered area. It's best sown in June when the weather is warmer. Don't allow the roots to get wet overnight or the plant will develop fungus. It should only be watered in the morning and allowed to dry out overnight.

Sorrel

Sorrel has a sour, strong flavor with a lemon hint to it. When it's cooked, it goes well with salmon and eggs, or it can be chopped and added to salads. It's easy to grow in containers, and more than one plant can be put in a pot. You should put it in a window box or sunny location with four hours of sun. Pick the outer leaves to keep it producing new inner leaves.

Chapter 4. The Right Pots for Your Plants

There are some things you'll need to get you going to get started in container gardening. The size of the containers you use will be determined by the kind of plants you would like to grow. Although there are many choices when it comes to containers and soil, my best piece of advice is to come up with a plan that you have for your container garden this year.

I also find that using your local gardening stores and online secondhand outlets list and Facebook marketplaces are good ways to find cost effective containers and gardening supplies. If you want your plants to grow healthy and to provide an abundance of fruit, then you need to ensure the container in which you plant them is big enough. The bigger, the better. Large plants need a lot of space, and most roots need room to grow.

Avoid small containers, as they often can't absorb sufficient water to get through hot summer days. Plus, the bigger your container, the more plants you can cultivate! Use containers, baskets, boxes, bathtubs, and other tubs, and troughs, anything that holds the soil. Just be sure that there are drainage holes in the bottom.

Caring recommendations for container gardening with vegetables in ceramic pots are they are generally more attractive than plastic pots, but plastic pots hold good moisture and will not dry out as rapidly as unglazed terracotta pots. Slip a plastic pot into a slightly larger clay one to get the best of both pots.

Black containers absorb heat when they're sitting in the sunlight. Most plants that grow in pots need to be watered as often as twice a day. Establish a container garden like in any other agribusiness company. The establishment of a container garden will begin with proper planning. Here are some different types of containers you will use to make smart decisions about what to plant in it.

Choosing Containers

The layout of the containers to be chosen and used is a demonstration of the design objectives set by the gardener on the basis of his/her bias and the availability of these materials.

With some talent, the native materials available in the locality can be transformed into gorgeously looking containers, like cut wooden poles or others. Only the imagination of the grower sets the boundaries. If the aim is to recycle and make long term use of objects that are usually dumped into the trash, then use old tires, sacks, soda cans, plastic bottles, etc.

The most readily available containers involve medium-sized plastic, much used only to hold ice cream or any other food products, and five-gallon transparent plastic containers that can be acquired from restaurants, bakeries, or marketplaces (wash containers with soap and warm water before use). The total depth and width of the container will be determined by what you plan to plant.

Container Types on the Basis of Material

Every element needs to be considered when choosing containers for your container garden. There is an almost endless number of professionally manufactured garden containers on the marketplace and an equivalent number of reprocessed products which could be turned into increasing containers. Growing product has its pro's and con's, and so each consideration must be acknowledged when determining which sorts of containers are worth investing in.

It is possible to use containers made of clay, wood, plastic, or metal for growing vegetables. Consider also the use of barrels, flowerpots, or hanging baskets. Unusual containers are going to add interest to your garden. Here are some of the most common garden container materials and a list of reasons to remember when making your decisions.

1. Terra-cotta Containers:

One of my favorite containers to plant. Terra-cotta containers are easily accessible in a variety of designs, shapes, and sizes, but those that are fired and/or glazed are less prone to flaking and breaking.

They look gorgeous in the garden, but they also have their major disadvantage as clay pots can also develop white salt blemishes on the outside and change color moss. Clay absorbs heat, too, a significant benefit in the spring, but not as effective in the summer when the atmosphere in the container can get too dry.

2. Ceramic Glazed Containers:

It is related to terra-cotta. They also look attractive and beautiful again in the garden, but they are also breakable. Ceramic glazed garden containers are available in many sizes, styles, designs, and colors. These are also made with the same fine textured clay that has been fired in a kiln and glazed with wires. They typically hold moisture a little better because of the glaze on the container, and, usually, won't get as hot as the terra-cotta containers.

3. Plastic:

During the last few decades, gardening through plastic containers and pots has come a significant way. By using the trendy shades and patterns, it allows the containers to appear more attractive. Plastic is supposed to be the easiest option, and the lightest one to shift around. As comparison with terra-cotta or ceramic pots, these plastic containers are very sturdy and much less likely to break. My only concern with plastic containers is they are considered as reusable, so

when you choose to buy them for your garden, ensure you utilize them year by year. Good insulation properties are seen in this type of container, as well as strong soil moisture retention. It's necessary to paint a high-quality exterior in order to restore their appearance.

4. Wood:

Especially in the case of planning your own wood garden, wood planter boxes are very affordable and easily accessible. Wooden containers, particularly raised bed containers, gives a lovely look in the garden. The casual, natural presentation of wood relates itself perfectly to both cottage-style gardens and residential landscapes.

Of course, rot resistant trees, such as redwood, cedar, or locust, make the best planters, while processed wood is often suitable for planters where no edibles are grown. Wood planters will eventually have to be repaired, but you're going to get rid of them several years before they do so. Wood is an ideal insulator, shielding the roots from harsh climatic variations in both summer and winter.

5. Cement Containers:

Cement planters are costly, but they are extremely durable. They're heavy, however, particularly once the soil has been added to them, so you're better off choosing more permanent containers which you don't intend to move around.

At the end of the day, almost anything can be turned into a container, and I love the unexpected options for bringing some character to your garden. The most important key point is that whatever you use, it is huge enough for your plants.

6. Window Box Container:

A large window box can create a handy salad within the reach of your arm! Whatever the size or type, place your containers where they are most convenient to be cared for and grow best. Many vegetables need 6 to 8 hours of direct sunlight to thrive and produce well. Plants in containers need the best soil, aeration, and drainage for healthy root growth and ideal harvesting.

Don't use soil from the garden; it is too heavy, it can become waterlogged, and it causes disease and insects. Alternatively, pick a good soilless mixture or use compost, either alone or in combination with a soilless mixture.

To keep plants growing, feed organic soil changes, including liquid seaweed, fish emulsion, or cow dung, on a weekly basis. Vegetables need moist soil continuously to ensure growth. All the following herbs and plants can do very well growing in window boxes and are a good choice for people living in town with limited living space.

Lettuce	Cilantro
Spinach	Sage
Mint	Cherry tomatoes

Basil	Strawberries
Nasturtiums	Bush/Hanging cucumbers

Holes/Drainage Preparation

Every container must have a sewage hole in the bottom so that the roots of the plant do not stand in the water. If there are no holes in the container, make at least four small nail holes on its sides ½ inch from the bottom.

All containers will require drainage holes to allow excess water to drain when the plants are watered. Roots allowed to stand in water are much more susceptible to infection and will sometimes rot and die. Tag three to five evenly spaced gaps at the bottom of the container and drill ¼ inch holes at these positions. The gaps will enable the surplus of water to drain. Often during watering, the potting medium will flow out of the drain holes.

Putting a piece of nylon window at the bottom of the pot can stop this from happening. Create a screen by putting the container at the top of the nylon window screen. Mark a location around the outside of the bottom of the container. Trim the ring out and put inside the container before adding the potting medium. The container is almost ready to be filled with a soilless potting medium. This medium is light in weight and comprises peat moss, a bog plant with great moisture removal. This can be bought from horticulture centers in bags and bulk, and from department stores in smaller quantities. This medium does not comprise nutrients, so you'll need to add moisture soluble fertilizers, such as fish emulsion, on a regular basis.

The benefit of soilless mixtures is that they are pasteurized and will be less likely to cause infection. Ten quarters of the dry mixture will be filled with about three medium-sized containers. The soilless coco fiber may be dusty and unpleasant, and therefore, it is best to moisturize the content before extracting it from the bag. It will also require a reasonable quantity of water and a vigorous mix with a clean trowel.

When only a small quantity is required, shift the required amount to a container before moistening. The moistened mixture could then be transferred to the planting container. Fill the container before the level of the mixture is around one inch below the upper edge of the container. This extra room enables the water to be collected before the mixture is slowly absorbed. Rub the surface softly smooth to even out the potting mixture. Once you've collected your plants, pot, soil, and fertilizer, cover the base with plastic screening the drainage hole so that your soil stays in and the water can get out of it.

Don't put mulch at the lower part of your pot, no matter what you've read. It isn't going to help with drainage but is simply going to make drainage worse. Fill the potting soil container to one inch or two from the top. Since your potting soil does not already have it, mix in fertilizer while carefully following the directions for quantity.

Organize the plants, bearing in mind the path your pot will be confronting. Dig a big hole for each plant, deep enough so that the top of the plant soil in its nursery pot is one inch or two from the top of the container. You do not want to hide the crown (where the stem joins the roots) of your plant with the soil. As well, you need enough space to keep it from splashing out of the pot when you're watering.

Fill the potting soil around your plants, again, being careful not to cover the crown. You would like to ensure that there is the soil around the roots of your plant and there are no air pockets. Water quietly and wisely, till the water goes out of the bottom of your pot.

Chapter 5.Growing Stra

Here are the most important things remember when it comes to container gardening:

Sun is key. Most of the herbs we nowadays use in cooking originate in the Mediterranean area and in places where the sun is plenty. Therefore, when you plant these herbs, you should make sure that you place them somewhere where they can get at least 8 hours of sun every day. With this being said, it may be better for you to keep these herbs outside, but if you can only keep them on the inside, make sure that the place where you put them is extremely well-lit. However, keep in mind the fact that you should not leave these plants in full daylight for too long because this can lead them to shrinking.

Great drainage, great size. This has been mentioned in numerous times before, but it is extremely important. Also, regarding pots, make sure that you plant more than 1-2 plants in a large pot because the soil will dry out differently there. Instead of using smaller pots, it may be better if you use larger ones.

Make sure that you have good soil. Planters discuss "soil," however for containers, it's really better to utilize something marked "potting blend," instead of anything named "potting soil." What is sold as "potting soil" is liable to be low quality and won't have the nutrients that your herbs need. "Potting blend" is made for the most part from natural matter, for example, at or composted plant matter, and intended to give container plants the surface area and the drainage that they require. Work with your herbs on occasion, but not often, or when they look pale and less than great. Never utilize substance-based fertilizers on the grounds that it can influence the taste of your herbs. Moreover, these sorts of fertilizers push speedy as opposed to moderate and sound development. Herbs that are developed excessively quickly frequently have less oils and flavors than those that developed more slowly. So, go simple when applying fertilizers. In the event that you planted with a decent, supplement filled potting blend, chances are you won't have to encourage your herbs regularly.

Compost can be important. Since you will be regularly watering the plants, there is a high chance that the compost you initially mix with the dirt will be washed out gradually. This means that you may have to renew the compost composition of the pot.

Pay attention to the roots. The root is obviously very important for the plant, so make sure you don't use compost that was mixed precisely to make the flowers grow. Also, do not collect the plants when they are blossoming and make sure that you don't uproot the plant when you collect the herb you need. Rather than do that, use a scissors to cut as much as you need out of it, leaving the root there.

Herbs that are alike should be planted together. Make sure that you never bring in the same pot two plants that require different conditions. For instance, some of them will need more water, while others will not like having too much water, so planting them together in the same pot will make them die out. Instead, keep the plants that require the same kind of conditions together and you will be able to take care of them with even less difficulty.

Some flowers live well with herbs. If you do a bit of research, you will find out that some edible flowers can be planted with herbs as well (at least as long as they require the same life conditions). This will add up some color and liveliness to your pots and containers.

You do need to prune your herbs. Pruning is very important for plants because it helps them develop better. Culinary herbs make no exception from this. The more you cut from them, the more they will develop from then on. When you harvest your herbs, make sure that you pick up 2/3 or at least ½ of the total so that there are some leaves left and the plant continues to grow.

Keeping all of these things in mind may sound difficult (and doing them may sound difficult as well). Of course, it will take a bit of time and learning if you want to succeed with this, but once you get things going everything will be extremely easy. Keep yourself positive because you are about to reap the benefits container gardening can bring into your life!

Water Is Also Important

As with every other living creature on the planet, container plants not only need water, they need a lot of it. Since they are confined to the smaller growing space of a container, it means that there is a limited amount of soil from which they can draw their moisture. Being in a container also means the soil dries out much easier and quicker.

You also have to keep in mind that being confined to a container means that even mild temperature changes, especially heat, affects these plants much more than plants that grow in the ground. Add in a lot of direct sunlight and this process speeds up even faster.

A common problem that beginner container gardeners make is trying to squeeze too many plants into a container. This means that there are now more plants fighting for the same limited water supply.

Some people will overcompensate by giving the plants too much water at one time with the belief that they will have it on hand when they need it. This is especially true if the gardener is going to be away for an extended period of time. Unfortunately, plants can only store so much moisture at a time.

The frequency with which you need to water a container garden depends on many factors. The type of planter being used, the size of the planter, the size of the plants, how long they have been planted, the time of year, etc. Getting into a habit of watering your plants on a regular basis is good, but it cannot be completely dependent upon as a reliable measure. Some days may be hotter than others. One day might have considerably more wind. This is why you are better off to have a system in place to do the deciding for you.

Another method is to choose what is called a self-watering planter. These containers have several openings located around the base a few inches from the bottom. They are watering ports to add water to the plant. As the plant dries out, the roots pull water from the bottom. However, in order to check the level of moisture, you will still need to stick a finger in the port to test the soil.

Prevention

It is always better to eliminate the possibility of problems before they have a chance to present themselves. While this is not always a 100-percent guarantee that you will be disease-free and bug-free, it will certainly go a long way in diminishing the number of problems that you have to deal with.

Rules of Prevention:

1. Keep an eye out. Since your containers are isolated from other growth, you should be able to spot pests and disease as soon as they appear. Catching an issue early gives you a much better opportunity of keeping it contained to a small area. When you water your plants, give them a once-over. If you use a self-watering system, get in the habit of inspecting them periodically.

2. Maintain a healthy garden. Plants are much more susceptible to disease when they are sick themselves. Keeping your plants healthy is one of the best preventive measures that you can practice. Keeping your plants well fed, with plenty of good, rich soil, and adequately watered will go far in helping fight off predators.

3. Start with healthy plants. Certain plants are more tolerant of some insects and diseases than others. Do some research to determine which varieties of plants are the hardiest. If you aren't sure when you are shopping for seedlings, ask a store associate. Sometimes, the information is given right on the plant's label.

4. Keep your tools clean. It's common for people to use their yard tools for more than maintaining their container garden. But moving them from fresh, potted soil to yard dirt can leave them open to picking up a wide range of unhealthy bacteria, fungus, and other nasty things. If you use your tools outside of your container garden, make sure to disinfect them thoroughly before using them again on your plants to avoid any kind of contamination.

Separate the good from the bad. If one plant comes down with a disease, chances are they all will unless you act quickly. Separate a plant at the first sign of trouble to avoid spreading it to others.

Treatment

Once bugs or disease hit, it's time to take action. The first thing people do is to run to their closest garden center and load up on chemicals. But wait! You want to make sure that you are stopping the infestation while limiting the residual damage left behind to the plants and the environment. How do you do that? Research.

In order to effectively deal with something, you have to know exactly what it is that you are being forced to deal with. Unless you are an expert in plant diseases and pests, you probably will not know what it is. Trying to describe a particular bug in detail or exactly what a specific kind of fungus or blight looks like to a garden associate might not be accurate enough. You need proof.

If you can, capture one of the bugs or pull off an infected leaf and take it with you for identification. If you can't or don't want to, get your hands on a pest, write down exactly what it looks like including shape, size, color, any distinguishing marks, if it flies, crawls fast, has long antennae, etc. And if that seems like too much work, take a picture or video using your cell phone. Now, your sales associate will know exactly what to give you to fight it.

If you are given a pesticide, make sure of a few details before purchasing. First, is it specifically designed for just this one problem or a host of problems? Many pesticides are designed to kill everything that moves. While this might sound reasonable to a gardener who is closely guarding their container garden, it also means that even good insects are being eradicated. This is not advisable.

There are pesticides that are only geared for specific pests. Going with these are always the best option.

Your second concern is its staying power. Does it quickly dissipate, or does it linger on the plant, and in the soil, for some time? If it hangs around, this means that a good rain will wash it out into the yard and who knows where else. If the pests are on your plant, you do not want pesticide flooding your yard.

Also, make sure not to try to use a chemical when there is even the slightest of wind since it will blow fumes or pesticide everywhere around you—including on you. And check the weather before you apply to ensure that a torrential downpour won't wash away your effort right after you apply it.

For those who wish to protect their plants while still keeping things healthy, there are natural alternatives. A little research will provide you with a list of natural, organic, and chemical-free alternatives that are proven to be effective while leaving the environment unscathed. Some of these might involve mixing certain commonly found household ingredients, but it's still better than putting out poison if it isn't necessary.

Chapter 6. Best Choices in Seeds

Conditions are a vital issue for every plant, even when it is in its seed form. In fact, seeds can be just as tricky as plants in terms of keeping them alive.

To avoid problems with faulty seeds or early failures with plants started from seeds, a lot of gardeners will do what is called "successive" plantings. This extends their harvest and also guarantees that they will at least get a few of the plants in question. Usually, they will use a journal to track dates when they start new pots or flats of seeds (most use a seven to fourteen-day gap between plantings) and will do two or more to ensure they get at least one good batch of plants.

They also do it to enjoy ongoing harvests or blooms. Consider that a container gardener may want to use a popular plant such as nasturtiums in their containers. They'll do this to eat the flowers, to add some incredibly bold color, and even as a way of trapping pests that feast on the tender foliage.

However, although nasturtium plants are quite durable and useful, to grow them from seed could be a waste of time and money if the gardener doesn't have the means of doing successive plantings and babysitting the plants until it is time to transplant.

So, what does this tell us about seeds and container gardening? Essentially, you can use seeds as a very economical way of obtaining certain plants, or to get ahead of the seasons and enjoy a longer harvest, but you have to have to work within the constraints created by the needs of seeds, the time to start them, and the best ways to handle (or not handle) them.

First Steps with Seeds

What we would suggest is that you begin your first year of container gardening with only a few plants that you might start from seed. For instance, you will want to invest in several packets of lettuces and greens because it is far more economical to grow them from seed instead of buying them in nursery flats.

On the other hand, you won't want to waste the time and money struggling to make heirloom tomato seeds grow and thrive before potting. And this is because more and more nurseries and garden centers make the finest heirloom and hybrids available, and always ready to pop right into the soil. And most container gardeners only need two to four strong plants to yield a huge crop of tomatoes.

How can you know exactly what to do about seeds versus plants? Ask yourself a few vital questions:

- How many of these plants do I need? If the answer is five or less, buy the plants.

- How much time do I have? If it is well into your local growing season, seek out the plants because seeds often take a few months to reach maturity and you may run out of time. Generally, seeds should be started a few weeks before your zone's last frost date. This is a date that you can get online from the USDA or from the National Oceanic and Atmospheric Administration's website. Also consider how long the seeds take to reach fruition (which can mean when they'll flower, make seeds, or produce food) as this is also an important issue - why spend the time and money if it is too late to see the end result?

- Am I committed enough to this sort of process? You have to invest in extra materials, spend a lot of time, manage conditions to create optimal settings, and be ready to really "baby" these baby plants...are you committed enough to this?

- Do I have the means? By "means" we are describing the financial resources to invest in the special seed starting medium, the pots, and any supplementary lights. We also mean the space and the time required as well.

- Am I an ambitious soul or am I more interested in guaranteed success? Trying to start digitalis and daylilies from seed is beyond the norm, but purchasing some packages of zinnias, nasturtiums, herbs, cucumbers, tomatoes, and squash is not a bad idea. If you are going for the ultimate in easy - stick with dwarf sunflowers as they are almost impossible to kill.

If it seems that seeds are the right way for you to begin some of your container gardening efforts, be sure that you have also considered the sunlight that your garden area will receive too. After all, when gardening indoors and starting seeds, you can control conditions. However, outdoors is an entirely different world and your once hearty seeds may falter.

A lot of new gardeners (those using containers or traditional beds) will want to know which plants are ideal for transplanting and which are good for starting from seed. Keep in mind that a lot of vegetables and some fruits do well if "direct seeded" into the soil in which they will be grown. This holds true of containers or garden soils. Others can transplant really well, and some are added to pots or the ground as "sets", cuttings, cloves, etc.

Best Choices in Seeds and Plants for Containers

To help you make the best choices, we have provided a list of the most common veggies and fruits capable of being grown in containers and identified the ways they are usually brought to life.

We have not mentioned flowers as that would require many pages. However, most gardeners opt for seedlings and plants in order to enjoy blooms in the first season, and most stick with bulbs, annuals, or hardy perennials instead of tender biennials:

Artichokes	Root divisions
Asparagus	One-year old roots
Basil	Transplant as seedling
Beans	Direct seed
Beets	Direct seed
Blueberries	One-year-old plants
Broccoli	Transplant as seedling
Brussels sprouts	Transplant as seedling
Cabbage	Transplant as seedling

Carrots	Direct seed
Cauliflower	Transplant as seedling
Celery	Transplant as seedling
Chard	Transplant as seedling
Chinese cabbage	Transplant as seedling
Chives	Transplant as seedling
Collards	Transplant as seedling
Corn	Direct seed
Cucumbers	Direct seed

Eggplant	Transplant as seedling
Endive	Transplant as seedling
Escarole	Transplant as seedling
Garlic	Direct seed
Garlic/shallots	Cloves
Herbs	Transplant as seedling
Horseradish	Root cuttings
Kale	Transplant as seedling
Kohlrabi	Transplant as seedling

Leeks	Transplant as seedling
Lettuce	Direct seed
Muskmelons	Direct seed
Mustard	Transplant as seedling
Okra	Direct seed
Okra	Transplant as seedling
Onions	Transplant as seedling
Onions	Sets
Parsley	Transplant as seedling

Parsnips	Direct seed
Peas	Direct seed
Peppers	Transplant as seedling
Potatoes	Seed potatoes
Pumpkins	Direct seed
Raspberries	One-year old canes
Radishes	Direct seed
Rhubarb	Root crowns
Rutabaga	Direct seed

Salad greens	Direct seed
Salsify	Direct seed
Squash	Direct seed
Sweet potatoes	Slips
Strawberries	One-year old crowns/plants
Tomatoes	Transplant as seedling
Turnips	Direct seed
Watermelon	Direct seed

Of course, you can try to grow everything from seed, and the biggest tip we could give you should you follow that route would be to plan ahead. Give yours seeds plenty of time to sprout and grow into strong seedlings that can be put outdoors as soon as possible.

Try to remember that you cannot grow a seedling in ideal conditions and then bring it directly outdoors. All seedlings have to have a period of "dampening" or "hardening" off. This is often done in a cold frame or by simply removing the seedlings from indoors and into a covered and sheltered place in the garden.

This does take time, and it also means that the seedlings will have to have a period of adjustment before they can once again grow and produce. Be sure that you read seed packets carefully to be sure that they are able to:

- Grow in your zone,

- Have enough time to become strong seedlings capable of transplant; and

- Have enough time remaining to enjoy a full growing season (all seeds have very clear information about their time from seed to produce)

Seed Starting and Re-Potting

How can you know when to start seeds and when to repot them into the containers? These are two entirely separate issues. So, let's begin with the issue of seed starting.

Before you even invest in a single packet of seeds you need to have the ideal "setup" for starting the seeds. While we could tell you that you must invest in the formal "seed starting trays" that come with fitted lids and which can hold a large number of seedlings, and that you must have proper heaters, etc., the reality is this:

You can start seeds in almost any vessel as long as the soil is correct.

Soil

Seeds cannot be exposed to any sort of fertilizers or harmful compounds, but you don't have to invest in costly bags marked as "seed starting mix". Instead, just whip up a batch of your own using equal parts of:

- Peat moss,

- Perlite, and

- Vermiculite.

A large five-gallon bucket is perfect for blending this mixture (be sure to drill several small holes in the bottom to use this also for moistening the mix before use as well).

You will want to moisten it and allow it to drain. Then you can put the mix into the seed starting trays or pots and moisten it again. After it has fully drained, it is time to plant the seeds, just be sure that your seeds are in the appropriate vessels for their needs.

Seed Starting Vessels

The vessels that you choose for seed starting will have to be selected based on the needs of the seedlings rather than on your personal preferences. For example, lettuce seedlings are fairly hardy and can be started in flats and then scooped out to be planted in a container.

Tomato seedlings, on the other hand, are not very happy about a lot of handling and it is best to start them in individual transplanting pots. You can make them from newspaper or purchase transplant pots from any nursery or gardening center.

The way to know which approach to use (flats versus pots) is dictated by the instructions on the seed packet. These always tell you how deep to plant a seed, how much spacing to leave between seeds, and how long to wait for germination.

The packets also indicate if the seeds have to be kept at a specific temperature to germinate or if regular room temperature conditions are acceptable. Many also indicate if the plants will benefit from being in a covered container - such as the plastic flats that are so commonly sold as seed starting kits.

However, a simple layer of plastic wrap placed lightly over the edge of the pot or flat can provide the same consistent moisture - just be sure that some aeration is occurring. Once seedlings reach the heights indicated on the seed packets, it is time to "harden" them off. This means you are going to get them ready for life outdoors. Most people begin by simply removing the plants from the greenhouse conditions of their seed flats. For instance, you might relocate seedlings from the covered flat or from beneath the grow light to a nearby windowsill. Be aware of things like overly cool drafts as these can easily kill tender seedlings but try to get them to a point halfway between total shelter and the natural world.

A few days of this and you can take them outdoors to harden up a bit further, just be ready to bring plants inside if a late frost is forecast. It takes a week to ten days for most seedlings to adjust, and then they can be put into their containers.

The best results, however, come from seedlings that were started in ideal conditions and which established themselves very well before hardening or dampening off. So, you can start seeds with a lot of things you have "on hand", but you can also invest in fail proof systems that create the ideal situation and setting for seed starting.

Chapter 7.Maintenance Tactics

You will need to maintain your container garden the same way you would do so for an in-the-ground garden. You just have to do so on a smaller scale.

How Do I Manage Pests and Diseases?

1. Regularly inspect your containers ~ Containers such as wooden planters can become weak over time, thus inviting pests like sow bugs and ants to come reside in them. As a result, they often damage your container more than the plant. When you see them present, remove them as soon as possible? Pests like these can-do extensive damage, sometimes making it necessary to transplant your plants to a different container.

2. Regularly inspect your plants ~ Be sure to check your vegetation for damage from insects. This will allow you to find what pests are causing the damage, remove them quickly, and prevent your plants from suffering major damage. You should be on the lookout for pests like snails and slugs. An easy trick for eliminating them is to simply place pieces of eggshells on the top of the soil. These pests find it extremely difficult to crawl over the rough surfaces and they will end up leaving.

Other pests such as aphids can be removed using strong sprays of water, followed by soapy water sprayed on bugs that are difficult to eliminate.

3. Get to know the pests commonly living in your area ~ While this will take some time to learn, this can prove to be time well spent. Some bugs are actually beneficial to you because they help get rid of the bad kind of pests. This means, if you don't know your bugs, you may end up eliminating the ones that you want to keep around. These good critters feed on bad insects such as aphids, as well as certain insects and pests.

4. Purchase new soil each year or sterilize the soil you plan to reuse ~ Diseases such as fungi and some insects can reside in the soil and debris in and around your containers. If your budget allows, purchase new soil each year when the time to start your garden comes. If money is tight, you could consider sterilizing the soil you already own; however, while it is cheaper to reuse your soil, it can be an extensive process.

5. Make sure the plants you have chosen to grow are native to your area ~ Some plants are more susceptible to pests and diseases than others, so it is especially important to avoid planting non-native types of plants in your containers. While some plants have managed to acquire their own natural resistance, many will fall prey to pests and diseases if they are not normally grown in your climate.

6. Know your soil ~ Be sure to check the soil in your containers regularly. Not only is it important to know if the soil is moist or dry, but you also want to dig down a little into the soil to check for bugs burrowed in the soil. Regular inspection will ward off infestation, making the solution easier to obtain.

7. Make sure your purchased plants are pest-free ~ When choosing plants, make sure that what you purchase are pest-free. If you accidentally purchase an infested plant, you may find it difficult or even impossible to get rid of the pests or diseases.

8. Maintain cleanliness in your garden ~ Get rid of dead plants as they can be a breeding ground for different pests and diseases.

9. Eliminate unhealthy plants from your containers ~ One of the best ways to protect your plants from pesky insects is to apply fertilizers that can help keep your plants healthy and less susceptible to various infestations. When your plant is nutrient-deficient, it becomes weak and can attract pesky insects. If there are weak plants, remove them instantly because they may be infected and susceptible to attracting pests.

A Few Treatment Methods

Because you are growing foods that you and your family will eat, it is best to think about organic and safe methods in treating pests and diseases. Below are just a few suggestions you can try:

-      Soft-bodied insects – Eliminate mealy bugs, mites and aphids by spraying a mixture of Ivory soap, canola oil and water. You can also use mineral oil, neem oil or hot peppers to burn insects.

-      Mites and other insects – You can make a spray bottle solution consisting of hot pepper sauce, Ivory soap and water.

- Fungal diseases – Create a mixture from baking soda and water. Spray the mixture on the affected plants until the fungal diseases disappear.

- Flying insects – Use garlic or onions and liquefy them in a vegetable oil tea.

- Snails and Slugs – Sprinkle crushed eggshells or lime in the soil area where the pests live.

- Fire ants and similar pests – Use citrus acid and molasses or a mixture of garlic and boiling water.

- Japanese beetles – Create a mixture out of water, liquid soap, canola oil and molasses. Pour the mixture in a can and place a rotten fruit in it. This creates a great trap for unwanted beetles.

It is important to note that these sprays do not just kill harmful insects, but also the good ones. Make sure that you use them selectively, and only spray the affected areas. It is also wise to spray in the morning and after a rain shower.

- If you are dealing with gnats, then it is wise to refrain from watering your crops for a while. Gnats cannot survive without water, and if you starve them, they will see your crop unfit for dwelling and disappear.

- If the stems and leaves of your crops are infested with bugs, you can cut them off. Prune the infested areas and throw them away. Some plants have the capacity to recover and sprout again regardless of how extreme your pruning is.

- Using flypapers is one of the best remedies to combat whiteflies and aphids. You can buy flypaper and use them to get rid of the insects. You can also make flypaper by using a yellow board that's coated with an adhesive. This will help eliminate a variety of pests that will be attracted to the board's color.

- You can also get rid of pesky insects by hand picking. Although this method is slow, it is extremely safe. You can do manual handpicking or use a handheld vacuum to get rid of pests.

What Are Some Common Mistakes I Should Know About?

Here is a list to make you more aware and better informed as a gardener as you tend your garden:

1. When dealing with large heavy containers, you wait for the end of the process before moving your pots ~ Do not make the mistake of filling up a large container with soil and your new plants and then try to move it. Put it where you want it to be and then proceed with filling it with soil and plants.

2. You forget to pay attention to proportions ~ A large container that is filled with stunted and stubby plants is going to look awkward. A good rule to incorporate into your gardening is to try to have at least one plant that will grow as tall as your container.

Once you have chosen one that will do this, you can plant other vegetation in the same container that are shorter and may even grow down the sides.

3. You drown your plants ~ Make sure your container has plenty of holes in the bottom so when you water, the excess water can drain out. Knowing when to water can be as simple as sticking your finger into the soil to see if it is dry or moist. If it feels dry to your fingertips, then it is probably time to give your plant a drink.

4. You deprive your plants of water ~ While overwatering your plant is not good, underwatering your plant is not any better. Many container gardens need watering at least once a day, especially during the summertime. For hanging plants or plants placed in small containers, they will need watering more than once a day because they have less soil to hold water and moisture. (See, I told you this could be tricky!)

5. You starve your plants ~ Potting mix is the most common ingredient used in container gardens. Unfortunately, these types of mixes don't usually contain enough nutrients for the plants to grow and flourish for the season. To compensate for the few nutrients potting mixes have, you will need to feed them fertilizers. There are many fertilizers to choose from, but the right kind will depend upon your choice of plants.

6. You are too cheap to buy good plants ~ Like everyone, you may be tempted to purchase plants you see in big box stores at cheap

prices because you think they will save you money. However, cheap doesn't always mean plants in good condition. Instead, try buying excellent quality plants from reputable stores because they are often healthier plants and have smaller chances of attracting diseases and pests. Reputable stores often offer a money-back guarantee if the plants prove to be diseased or die.

7. You do not have realistic expectations ~ If you are away from home a great deal, you need to consider a self-watering system or enlist the help of a neighbor or family member. Also, consider your living style and personality.

8. You are afraid to prune your plants ~ It is ironic that some plants do best when we cut off limbs. Tomato plants are like this. If you have too many branches, some of the plant's energy is expended on growing branches rather than producing fruit.

9. You fill a large container with 100% potting soil ~ If you are planning to grow shallow-rooted plants in a huge pot, try not to fill it with potting soil because it can be very expensive. Instead, fill in the bottom of the container with empty bottles, rocks or anything that can take up space.

10. You use the wrong sized container ~ Container gardening is not one of the many things that you can do mindlessly or without careful planning. Do not grow shorter plants in a huge pot as it can look stunted or plant vegetable varieties in a small pot. Make sure that you choose a container with a height and size that is proportionate to the number of plants that you want to grow as

well as with the size of the plant. If a crop will eventually grow tall, then choose an elongated container.

11. You use containers with little to no drainage holes ~ There are pots that are sold without holes or with a limited number of drainage holes. Refrain from using these pots because they can keep your soil too moist. This can result in rotting of the roots and death of the plant since there are no holes for excess water to drain out. Make sure you take the time to drill enough holes to let water drain out and to let the roots have room to breathe and grow.

12. You recycle unsterilized containers ~ You should not reuse your old containers without making sure they have been disinfected first. Wash the containers with soap and rinse with water or hydrogen peroxide. This will terminate bacterial growth and prevent them from infecting the plants you are planning to grow.

13. You use disease-carrying gardening tools ~ Failure to disinfect gardening tools can increase the chance of spreading pests and plant diseases. This is especially true if you have certain areas in your garden that are infested. Make sure that you thoroughly disinfect your forks, shovels, pruning shear blades, rake tongs, trowels, digging tools and other gardening equipment before you use any of them on other plants.

Chapter 8. Companion Planting

Companion planting is the act of growing different plants together so that the plants could benefit one another by improving their health and final yields. It is not a new practice. It has been in existence as far back as when Native Americans were using the 3-sisters method (which is an ancient Cherokee Indian practice). The practice has, however, been modified through observations and careful studies. Some plants attract beneficial insects, and when these plants are grown with a compatible companion, the insects help to protect the companion. Pest control is arguably the most significant benefit of this practice. It utilizes the natural effect of herbs in repelling pests from attacking other plants. With companion planting, there is no need for the use of insecticide or pesticides. The herbs planted helps to attract beneficial insects such as ladybugs, lacewings, parasitic wasp, pirate bug, leaf miner parasite, etc. The important thing to note about companion planting is that not all plants can accommodate one another. Therefore, it takes knowing which plants to grow with each other and which ones should be far apart from each other to get the desired result. For example, plants that majorly feed on the same type of nutrient should not be planted together because it creates a situation where both plants struggle and fight for survival. It may even happen that neither of the plants in this situation will eventually produce good yields as a result of insufficient nutrients intake.

An example of a perfect choice for companion planting is a combination of tomatoes and carrots or a combination of radishes and green onions. It is also recommended to choose companion plants according to your garden's maintenance requirements.

Natural Support

Natural support is provided to low plants like potatoes, peas, squash, etc. by tall plants such as sunflowers, corn, etc. When you grow climbers like beans with tall plants like corn, there is no further need for reinforcement because the beans will use the corn as a climbing pole.

Healthy Soil

By planting compatible plants together, it creates a healthy growing environment for the plants. Some vegetable plants are known to improve the soil quality of other plants.

Pest Control

Growing crop together helps to control pests. For instance, when you plant corn and then add beans with squash to it, the beans supply nitrogen to the corn, the squash prevents weed from growing while the squash and beans climb the corn for support, and they all repel one another's pests.

Encourage Beneficial Insect that Aids Pollination

Companion planting will help to attract beneficial insects in your garden, and when these insects spend more time in your garden, they aid pollination. Insects like bees, birds, butterflies, etc. are agents of pollination that companion planting promotes. Several flowers like Marigolds are known to improve plants' growth and also repel several pests.

Increased Productivity and Improved Flavors of individual Plants

The benefits associated with growing of plants' varieties together all work to bring about increased productivity. Companion planting also improves the flavors of different plants. An example of this is the case of basil and lettuce or tomatoes.

Access to Growing More Varieties

Companion planting also makes it possible for you to grow several types of a particular plant. You can cultivate different kinds of tomatoes, peas, and almost any kind of plant in your garden.

Saves Space

This practice saves garden space and helps you get optimum benefit from your yard, no matter how small it is. You can plant fast-growing crops with slow-growing ones or grow small plants under tall ones or grow plants in close proximity.

Some examples of plants you can grow together are below:

- Chives are a great companion with vegetables. They help to drive away aphids, beetles, and enhance the growth of carrots.

- Basil is an excellent companion for most vegetables as well. It helps to improve the flavor of the plants grown with it. Basil is especially great with tomatoes.

- Sage is a perfect match with cabbage, carrots, and rosemary but not compatible with cucumbers. It helps to repel moths and flies.

- You could try out peppermint with vegetables, especially tomatoes. Mint keeps pests like mosquitoes, aphids, and ants far away and attracts beneficial insects like bees.

- Chamomile is also a great match with vegetables. It helps to attract beneficial insects and pollinators to your garden as well as improve the flavors of vegetables or other herbs planted alongside it.

- When you plant comfrey with tomatoes and other fruiting vegetables, it will enhance the soil nutrients. Also, try growing thyme with cabbage or similar herbs. It will help to repel worms and benefit the companion plant.

- Marigold helps to repel leafhoppers, worms, beetles, and nematodes and makes a great companion with vegetables and herbs. An interesting thing about Marigold is perhaps how it releases chemicals that act as a toxin in the plants' roots and uses it to fight pests like mole crickets.

- Lavender is a perfect companion plant for fruits like blueberries and most herbs. It attracts beneficial insects as well as pollinators.

The many benefits associated with Companion planting are the reasons the practice is widely accepted and commonly used today. If you are yet to take advantage of companion planting, there is no better time than now to begin and get the maximum benefit from your garden. You can always experiment with plants to see which ones compatible and which ones are are not. Remember that there is no crime in experimenting and trying things out in your garden. You can easily make necessary adjustments when you notice plants that are not doing so well together. No matter how big or small your container garden is, endeavor to grow different plants together as this will help you to get the best possible results from your garden.

Chapter 9. Vertical Gardening

What is Vertical Gardening?

Imagine if you would, a world where vegetables and fruit all climb, twine and grow upward, creating beautiful and landscapes that save space, produce high yields, require less effort, and reduce pest and disease problems. Whether your goal is self-reliance or the simple satisfaction of growing your own foods, a bountiful vegetable and fruit harvest can be yours regardless of the amount of space you have. I'll show you how to transform whatever available space you have into grow-up or grow-down gardens with just a few inexpensive supplies that you may even be able to get for free, if you know where to look. Vertical gardening is a contemporary, highly productive and nearly effortless, growing system that uses a wide variety of plants in both small and large garden spaces. There are hundreds of varieties of vegetables and fruits that are perfect vertical gardening.

One of the greatest achievements of vertical gardening is that it almost guarantees better results from day one, by reducing both the amount of space required and the work needed to prepare new beds. A bush variety, by contrast, will exhaust itself as little as two weeks.

What Are the Benefits of Growing Vertically?

Growing vegetables vertically will forever change the way you normally think of growing plants in rows and beds. If you're one of the millions of people who want to experience gardening for the first time, one of the millions of gardeners looking for easier and more rewarding ways to garden, or one of the millions of gardeners who have given up all hope of gardening because of substandard results, consider some of the incredible benefits vertical gardening:

- Growing plants up instead of out uses less resources and a much smaller footprint
- Digging from Day 1 or no to little soil preparation
- Superior air circulation and less risk of plant diseases and infestations
- Easier harvesting, no more searching row by row of plants for the few vegetables that are ripe
- Larger yields in less space

Vertical gardens can, under the right conditions, be planted at any time of the year and can bear a harvest year-round. From seasonal planting this unbinds you and affords you the ability to have your favorite out of season produce at your fingertips.

The biggest mistake gardeners make in planting a garden is starting too large. After digging the soil in a large plot and planting a traditional garden in long, straight rows, summer days get hot and humid, encouraging a daily onslaught of weeds and creating a daily need for plant watering and it becomes a challenge to find enough time to tend to the garden on a daily basis.

What are the Disadvantages to Vertical Gardening?

A vertical garden is removed from the ground level, "natural" soil, and as such it is not allowed some of the perks that come with a traditional garden. Vertical gardens are much more easily affected by temperature than a traditional garden. A traditional garden has a vast surface area in which to spread out temperature changes, and as such has a relatively constant temperature throughout the day. Afforded a wider root system, Traditional garden plants are also that can spread out and pull nutrients and water from the surrounding soil, while a vertical garden is limited to only the soil in its "pocket." With this being the case, you must be vigilant in watering your vertical garden, and you must also use a liquid fertilizer or a compost tea on your garden frequently. In hot months with a lot of sun, this may require you to water your vertical garden a minimum of once per day.

What Can be Used to Create a Vertical Garden?

The beauty of vertical gardening is that almost anything can be used to create your garden. Many household items that we carelessly toss away can be turned into a vertical garden. Some items that I have used to create vertical gardens include:

- Old soda bottles (they work great to grow herbs in on your windowsill)
- 5-gallon buckets left over from home renovations
- 50-gal drums (just make sure they are really well cleaned out and, if you can, should contained food grade materials)
- Wooden barrels
- Traditional flowerpots be they plastic, ceramic or terracotta, work fantastically (you can purchase or make your own stand to increase the amount of gardening space you have).
- Gutter systems that were old. Basically, anything that can hold soil can be turned into a garden. Vertical gardening is a perfect solution for the gardener on a budget

When Growing Vertical it is Important to Be Creative in Your Planning

Containers, shelves, and hanging baskets combination works really well to create a complete garden in a small space such as a patio or balcony.

If you can tackle a project like building a frame with cross-supports and built-in shelves, this also works quite well and can be an attractive feature in your landscape or on the deck or patio.

Below are the plans for my personal favorite vertical garden Do-It-Yourself. Feel free to make it your own and take this idea. Like I said, if it can hold soil, plants can grow in it.

Plants that Thrive in Vertical Vegetable Garden

Now that you know how to build a vertical garden, what exactly should you plant in it?

The vegetables listed below are great candidates for any space-saving garden. Simply plant seedling or seeds as usual but remember to install the support at the time of planting. Attempting to install the support system at a later time will be much more difficult, and more than likely cause damage to the plants root system and vines. (I unfortunately learned this the hard way!)

Climbing Plants:

- Cucumber

- Squash (Acorn or Butternut)
- Tomato

- Green Beans
- Peas

- Lima Beans

Each of these will need support system such as trellis or frame to climb upward.

Non-Climbing Plants:

- Lettuce

- Radishes

- Peppers

- Onions

- Eggplant

- Potato (Regular or Sweet Potato in a container)
- Parsley

- Herbs

These can be included in any vertical garden and do not need a support system.

Where is it best to Grow Up?

As with any garden, finding the best location for growing is one of the most important keys to your success.

- The majority of vegetable plants require a minimum of 6 hours of sunlight per day.
- Place your garden near a convenient source of water. With proper advanced planning, you can design your garden so that all you need to do is turn on the faucet for a few minutes to provide adequate water to all of your plants.

- Stay away from trees and shrubs. They will compete with your garden for water and shade your plants.
- Locate your garden facing south if possible; this will ensure that they receive ample sunlight.

If you do not have access to a sunny location, broad leafy vegetables will grow quite well in shade or partial shade.

Choose your favorite vegetables for your first vertical garden. Doing so will make all of your labor much more rewarding as the end result will be vegetables that you love to eat. Start small to avoid becoming overwhelmed. Remember that each year, as your skills grow, you can add more plants and varieties

One of the best features about using a vertical or container garden is that, if you decide to plant indoors, be it in a garage, spare bedroom, or even a simple closet, all seasonal planting can be disregarded. That's right, since you control the temperature in your home, you can help to maintain opportune growing temperatures for your edibles! You don't even need to have sunlight to produce great vegetables for your family by utilizing growing lights. You can even create your own for just a fraction of the cost with a bit of ingenuity. Should you choose this route, you need to make sure that either by window or artificial lighting, you are still giving your plant the correct amount of light each day. You will also want to check to see if desired humidity is in your plant range and you may need to adjust in your growing area accordingly the humidity. An improvised greenhouse and a humidifier can help to keep your indoor planting from affecting the rest of your house. If you choose multiple smaller containers that remain portable, you can create a hybrid garden that you can move outside during opportune growing weather and, should the weather turn inclement, you can move quickly the planters indoors to a safe growing environment. If you decide to use container or create a vertical garden, you want to make sure to follow these 5 key steps to maintain a healthy garden.

5 key steps to help a garden Grow UP healthy:

- Water daily
- Fertilize often
- 6 hours of sunlight MINIMUM
- Start with a good soil
- Use plenty of compost

Chapter 10. What You Need to Know About Fertilizers

The drawback of planting in pots is that they will have lesser amounts of nutrients in the soil. They will also hold less water compared to garden beds. Because of this, you have to make sure you maintain the water and nutrient levels in the soil. You will need to this on a regular basis. This will help the plants survive and grow healthy flowers and leaves. It will also make sure the plants produce edible vegetables. You should be aware of a few things you need to do to maintain your garden. This includes feeding the soil, avoiding soil compaction, and pruning or caging.

Whether you're growing your plants inside or outside, you have to fertilize in order to be successful. The best way to go about this is to prepare a nutrient solution and pour it over the soil mix. The fertilizer is then absorbed by the roots and adds what's missing to them. Even if the potting mix is perfect from the start, it's soon going to be depleted because they're constantly used up by the plants. The faster the plant grows the more fertilizer and water it's going to need. Consequently, while water increases, the more nutrients are lost.

When you add fertilizer to potted plants, always opt for an organic brand. They are just as effective as the chemicals and they won't burn the plant. They also supply a wide range of micronutrients, minerals, vitamins, and amino acids to the plant.

When you fertilize is actually important, too. Plant nutrient has to change with the different stages of growth. For example, to get the most out of annual plants, you want to start them on high nitrogen fertilizer to promote leaf development and then switch to high phosphorous, low nitrogen solution to encourage them to bloom and produce fruit.

If you don't know how to purchase fertilizer, take a look at some of the following information.

There are three numbers on every package of fertilizer. They're always in the same order and they stand for the percentage of weight of N-P-K or Nitrogen, Phosphorous, and Potassium. These are all necessary for healthy plants.

For example, all-purpose fertilizer might have a ratio of 5-5-5. The first number is nitrogen, which helps your plant develop green growth and protects the plant's overall health. Fertilizers high in nitrogen are good for leafy vegetables like Swiss chard and lettuce. Natural sources include liquid fish emulsion and blood meal.

The second number is phosphorus. Blooming plants, such as peppers and tomatoes, will benefit from a fertilizer rich in phosphorus. Organic fertilizers that have phosphorous contain bone meal and seabird guano.

The third number is potassium, and this is for the stem growth and overall plant health. It's used on root crops like beets, carrots, potatoes, and on young trees in the fall. Sources of organic potassium are greensand and many liquid fertilizers.

Plants can absorb nutrients through both roots and leaf pores. Foliar feeding will supply nutrients to the plants immediately. It's great for fast growing plants such as vegetables and should be used as an extra boost during the growing season. Only use fertilizers rated for foliar feeding, or you could burn the leaves.

Feeding the Soil

Earlier we talked about how to prepare the soil with organic fertilizers such as compost and manure. In the last topic we learn how to rotate your crops through the growing season to keep the soil nutrient rich. Sometimes, though, this is not enough to keep the soil healthy. If this is the case, you will need to feed the soil. As with anything else, your plants will tell you if they are getting enough nutrients. If they appear weak or stunted, or if they are not yielding as many veggies as you expected, the soil might be losing nutrients.

If this is the case, you should feed the soil. I recommend using organic methods, just as when you prepared the soil. To do this, you will need manure or compost and a small garden fork. When the soil in the pot is moist, break up the upper layer (four to six inches) with the garden fork. Then, till (or mix) the compost or manure into this layer, again with the garden fork. When you are done, spread more on top of the soil. Then water the plant well.

You can also use store-bought plant feed. Garden centers have organic plant food for sale. You should try to use these if you can. Most of these kinds of feed should be mixed with water before you apply them. Then, when you water your plants, you are also feeding them.

Soil Compaction

Just like in a garden bed, it is important to prevent the soil in your pots from being compacted. One way this happens is by leaning your weight on the soil when you are gardening. This is more common in garden beds. Gardeners will kneel or walk on their beds, which crushes the soil underfoot. But it can happen in large planters as well. Be careful not to compact the soil in this way.

A more common way soil is compacted in pots is by watering. If you do not use a watering can that has a rose to break up the water, or if you do not use a nozzle on your hose that makes a fine mist, you risk pounding the soil into a hard crust. Of course, the best way to prevent this is by using the proper tools. But if you do not have these kinds of tools, there is another solution. You can place a broken pot or plate in the soil. Then, let the water flow onto the hard surface. This will lessen the force of the water before it touches the soil.

Before you water your plants, you should also break up the soil. You can do this with a fork or a trowel. Doing this will allow water and air to pass more easily to the roots.

Pruning and Caging

Many of your plants should not be left to grow however they want. You will have to control their growth with stakes, cages, or pruning.

Big, bushy plants like tomatoes, peppers, and squash need stakes and cages. This is true even if you are growing patio varieties. The cage or stake will support the plants. This will be especially important when they begin to produce their heavy fruit. Without a support structure, the fruit will drag the plant's branches to the ground. Place cages around tomatoes and peppers early. You will need to guide the plants up into the cage as they grow. This will be much easier than trying to force a cage over a plant that has already grown and is too bushy.

Pruning makes sure plants do not grow out of control. It also promotes the kind of growth you want. For example, you should prune tomato plants. You will want to pinch the stems that grow at 45-degree angles from the main stem. Leave the stems that grow at right angles to to the main stem. The 45-degree stems take nutrients away from any tomatoes growing on that stem. Leaving them on will result in many tomatoes not becoming ripe. Talk to a master gardener about what kinds of pruning the other veggies in your garden need.

Chapter 11. Storing and Preserving Your Harvest

Storing Your Harvest

Storing your harvest is the best means of dealing with the surpluses of your crops against season when little is growing. The different ways to store your vegetables include freezing, drying and preserving. Some vegetables and fruits store well for months if you keep them in the appropriate conditions. What is most important is selecting unblemished variety and inspect them frequently, taking out any contaminated items. For instance, one spoiled pear can damage the entire bunch. Storing the harvests in a dehydrated, well-ventilated environment would prevent them from decaying. You can use a shallow cardboard box or wooden crate as well as storage boxes. Whichever you are using, ensure it gives room for proper ventilation.

Pears and apples are suitable for storing. Cover each fruit in paper and put in separately in the base of your container. Root vegetables like beets, potatoes, and carrots also suitable for storing. Remove the leafy edge of the carrots and beets put them in the box separately without covering. They both have the advantage of being covered by a layer of sand, making them tough. Potatoes could be stored in paper sack or hessian. Harvest them on a dry day and allow drying in sun. Take away any mire from the potatoes to stop from forming mold. Store them in a dark area to prevent from forming poisonous green patches on the outer layer. Leave parsnips in the ground over the winter and harvest when you need them.

Shallots, Garlic, and onions are to be dried thoroughly and plaited before storing in a dry environment. The tops could also be removed and hang the bulbs in an old pair of netting or tights. Squash related plants like pumpkins can stay for about three months. It all depends on the type. Do not keep marrows and pumpkins after mid-winter. However, other squash like spaghetti and butternut can be kept till early spring. Make sure they are in perfect state and store them in a dry, cool area like in the cabinet. A crop like zucchini doesn't stay long but can be refrigerated for about three weeks.

Leafy plants like spinach and lettuce don't store well, and they are ideal to be eaten in a few days of harvest. Plant more often in the early fall for you to have something to harvest in the cold periods. Legumes like beans and peas could be blanched and frozen or dried for use in a stew.

Freezing Your Harvest

Freezing is an easy and quick means to preserve your harvest. Freeze in usable sizes so the frozen crops can quickly defrost when using. Select only ripe vegetables and fruits and freeze them immediately after harvesting. Put them in a plastic container or a sealed freezer bag to guarantee they are well kept and do not undergo freezer burn. Some vegetables and fruits will require blanching before freezing to prevent water in them rupturing and crystallizing their cell walls, leading to a soft consistency and boggy when defrosted. Just plunge the vegetable into a big bowl of boiling water at least ⅓ of the normal cooking time, and move to chilled water, before patting dry and freezing.

The following freeze perfectly well:

- Gooseberries
- Rhubarb
- Cranberries
- Peas
- Blanched beans (these include French and runner)
- Blanched apples
- Blueberries
- Raspberries

Drying, Pickling and Bottling Your Harvest

Crops that dry better are apples, peppers, and tomatoes. Drying could considerably change the texture and taste of your products and could make appealing additions to meals. Just clean and thinly cut your vegetables and fruits and place the pieces in a single layer on a baking tray. You usually leave it outside or sun to dry it out. You can use your oven to dry it, put your oven to its minimum temperature set and place the tray inside for some hours until pieces have dried up. Following that, store the bits in a sterile airtight container and eat within one or two weeks.

Shallots and beets are tasty after pickled and can be kept for some months. Clean and prepare beets (do not take out the tops closer to the root, as it could lead to leaching out of color). Put in boiling water for about thirty minutes or until the heads and skins can be easily rubbed off. Cut them and put in a sterile jar and wrap in pickling vinegar. For shallots, peel and trim the bottom and tops. Put them inside a shallow plate and cover with salt to draw out surplus moisture. Leave them all night and clean carefully and put in a sterile jar then wrap with pickling vinegar.

How to Use Preserved and Dried Herbs

There are several ways to use preserved herbs. You can use herbs in cooking, flavoring, aromatherapy, as medicinal plants and for crafts and DIY purposes. The possibilities with herbs are endless, as long as you use your creativity and imagination to discover new ways to use preserved and dried herbs. Meanwhile, here are some suggestions to get you started.

Home Decoration and Gift Ideas

Kitchen Wreath – wreaths are lovely decorations for all seasons, but an herbal kitchen wreath is great during autumn or winter. Here's how to make one:

You'll need:

Grapevine wreath

Floral wire

Herbs of your choice

Padding wire

Ribbons

To make:

Take the grapevine wreath and choose one herb that you will use as a base for the wreath. Wrap and arrange it around the grapevine and secure with padding wire. Next, take smaller herbs like dried lavender flowers and attach a floral wire to its stems. Then, insert it into the wreath and secure by twisting and wrapping the floral wire around the grapevine. Repeat for the other herbs. You can use a ribbon to tie and hang the wreath on your door.

Herb Collage – create your own artwork by using dried herb leaves and flowers

You'll need:

Herbs of your choice

Picture frame

Construction paper

Craft Glue

To make:

Take the construction paper and the herbs. Arrange the herbs in the construction paper and use glue to permanently stick them to the paper. Let dry. Take the picture frame and put your herb collage in it. Hang and display.

Scented Pillows – scented pillows are very relaxing and great decorations for your living room or bedroom.

You'll need:

2 lbs. dry herbs of your choice

Pillowcase

To make:

Take the dry herbs and fill the pillowcase with them. After filling the pillowcase, sew the edges shut. You can tie a ribbon around it for decoration or leave it as it is.

Note: Instead of using only one type of dried herb, try combining different herbs for a pillow with assorted scents. This pillow can be used for aromatherapy and treating headaches.

Scented Jars – this easy DIY décor is perfect for recycling pint jars. The jars can be used to freshen and scent up a room or as a centerpiece for a table in the living room, dining area or the kitchen. You can even use this a candle holder.

You'll need:

Pint jars

Herbs of your choice and some citrus fruits like orange or lemon

Water

Ribbons

Labels or gift tags (optional)

Candle (optional)

To Make:

Take a pint jar and fill it with herbs and citrus fruits. Fill ¾ of the jar with water. Close the lid of the jar and freeze for 2 weeks. After 2 weeks, take the jar and let it thaw. Once the water is melted you can use the scented jars. Tie a ribbon and add labels for decoration or you can open up the jars and put a floating candle in.

Note: You can also freeze the scent jar without water.

Herbal Christmas Ornaments – dry herbs can be used to make Christmas ornaments like topiary and spheres. It adds a unique touch to your decorations and ornaments while scenting up your room.

You'll need:

Styrofoam ball of any size

A cup of different dry herbs

Waxed paper

White glue

Greening pins

Ribbons

To make:

Pour the dry herbs into a big bowl. Crush the dried herbs into smaller pieces. This will give your ornaments a smoother texture. Then, take the Styrofoam and coat an area with glue. Dip this area into the herbs. Press and let dry before repeating the process in other parts of the ball until it is completely covered with herbs. Place the coated balls in wax paper and roll the balls until the herbs firmly press into the ball. Take a ribbon and attach it to the ornaments by securing with a greening pin.

You can try combining different herbs to create an ornament with different colors. If you're up to the challenge, use the white glue to form shapes in the Styrofoam before dipping it in the herbs. This will create an interesting pattern and design for your ornaments.

Chapter 12. Organic Sprays

There are many chemical sprays available today that will rid you of these pests. However, by far the most effective is to cover the plants with a horticultural fleece.

This admits enough light for photosynthesis to take place but denies access to butterflies and other flying critters like greenfly.

Alternatively form a simple frame over them and lay over butterfly mesh – making sure that the mesh is not laying on the leaves thereby giving access to the egg-laying butterflies!

Organic Sprays

There are many ways to control pests without the need for chemical sprays. Both home-made and store-bought solutions are readily at hand in the battle against creepy-crawlies of all descriptions!

First of all, it is always good to keep in supply a number of hand-held sprayers. Once these are clearly labelled then they can be on hand and ready for use.

These sprays are good for controlling aphids, caterpillars, greenfly, blackfly and many other soft bodied insects. As a general rule do not spray before heavy rain is forecast, and always spray topside and underneath the leaves as well as the stem of the plant.

Home-Made Solutions

Garlic water spray:

Add one or two large cloves of garlic peeled and chopped in half, to a 1-pint spray container and leave for 2-3 days to infuse. Spray the plant liberally to kill the bugs.

This spray also makes a good fungal treatment for your plants, effective against powdery mildew, and will deter many species of insects.

Lemon rind spray:

Peel the rind from two large lemons and add to 1 pint of boiling water. Stir and leave to cool before spraying on your plants.

This is very effective against aphids and gooseberry sawfly.

Vinegar Spray:

Fill your water spray bottle ¾ full of water and the rest with distilled white vinegar. This will kill aphids and larvae on contact, and other critters over a short time.

Test a small area though, at least a day before you use it on the whole plant as some plants will react badly to the acetic acid in the vinegar. If so, try diluting the mixture.

Hot Pepper spray:

Chop a few hot peppers into your spray bottle and leave to infuse with water for a few days. Spray directly onto the insects.

This is a general-purpose spray that is very effective against a whole range of bugs.

Be careful not to get any in your eyes though!

The Bug Bomb!

This is a bug-busting spray that can be extremely effective against aphids and most leaf-chewers in general.

Combining the hot pepper with the garlic deterrent ensures a good all-round deterrent, whilst the liquid soap clings to the plant giving it a longer active lifespan.

Check it out on a small surface before use though – just in case the plant cannot tolerate it well. And remember to protect your skin and eyes from the spray.

Take about 1 quart of water and chop one garlic bulb into four pieces and add to the liquid.

Add a teaspoon of cayenne pepper, one hot chilli (chopped).

Mix thoroughly and let steep for about 4 hours. Strain the liquid through cheesecloth or similar and add 1 tablespoon of liquid soap to the mixture.

Store for a few days to infuse before use.

Apple Cider & Herb Spray:

This was a concoction allegedly used in medieval times to ward off the black death – and apparently it worked!

Stinks like blazes whilst it is still wet, but the smell soon retreats as it dries. This makes a good general insect repellent – but test on plants first to be sure they do not get damaged by the vinegar.

Add the following ingredients to 1 quart (2 pints) of water.

1 – 32oz apple cider vinegar.

2 TBSP each of dried Sage, Rosemary, Lavender, Thyme and Mint.

Add two cloves.

Mix thoroughly and leave for two weeks in an air-tight container, before straining out the liquid and adding to your hand sprayer.

Geranium Spray:

The smell of geraniums is known to chase away many destructive insects, and so this mixture can make a good deterrent spray and is generally well tolerated by the plants.

Take a large bunch of geranium clippings and place into a blender with about 1 pint of water. Blend until smooth then strain the liquid through a fine strainer.

Add about 1 tablespoon of the liquid to a 1-pint hand sprayer and spray the plants thoroughly.

This idea will also work with a garlic or marigold substitute.

Horseradish Insecticide:

Bring 3 quarts of water to the boil; add 2 cups of cayenne peppers, a 1-inch piece of chopped horseradish root. Add 2 cups of packed scented geranium leaves (if you have them but not essential). Let mixture steep for 1 hour, cool, strain and spray.

This is effective against Aphids, blister beetles, caterpillars, Colorado beetles, whiteflies and other soft-bodied insects.

Store-Bought Solutions:

Food-Grade Diatomaceous Earth: This is a natural product made from tiny crushed fossilized water plants. It is very effective against a number of plant predators including sawfly, coddling moth, twig borer, thrips, mites, cockroach, cutworms, slugs, snails and many other insects.

This food-grade diatomaceous earth is non-toxic to animals and humans so is safe to use. It can also be mixed with water and sprayed to get the underside of the leaves. Do not spread on flowering plants as this earth is an indiscriminate killer of many insects – including friendly pollinators.

Insecticidal Soap:

Not to be confused with herbicidal soap – which will effectively kill your plants! Insecticidal soup is mixed with water and sprayed directly onto the insects to kill them.

This only works whilst the spray is wet and by direct contact with the bugs. Mix a solution of about 1 tablespoon of liquid to your plant sprayer and spray a few infested leaves. Wait for a day or two to be sure the plant suffers no ill effects, before spraying the rest of the plant.

This is effective against most soft-bodied bugs such as aphids, and the early larvae of other tougher bugs.

Derris Dust:

Although this is a naturally occurring compound from tropical vine and other plants (active ingredient rotenone), there is some debate as to the wisdom of using it as it can be slightly toxic to humans and animals if accidently ingested.

It is however very effective against leaf-chewing caterpillars, potato beetles, cucumber beetles, flea beetles, cabbage worms, earwigs, raspberry beetles, and asparagus beetles.

The powder should be scattered onto or around the affected area as the bugs will die upon making contact with it. As in the case with diatomaceous earth, do not spread on flowering plants.

As an added precaution, food should not be harvested within two weeks, and should be thoroughly washed before use.

Neem Oil:

This is mixed with water according to the instructions and sprayed onto the plant to remove sucking pests such as spider mite and aphids.

Nosema locustae:

This is organic bait which can be purchased. This affects the digestive system of the grasshopper leading to death. When healthy grasshoppers consume their dead friends, they too will become sick and die.

Conclusion

Some people are discouraged from growing their own vegetables because they do not have a garden, or a plot of land big enough to raise vegetables on. This is however a misapprehension, as the fact is that by following the right guidance you can provide a good supply of vegetables from a very limited space by utilizing the ideas in this manual.

Growing vegetables in containers I believe is becoming more popular, especially amongst city-dwellers who do not have acres of land to work, but perhaps have a balcony or terrace at their disposal.

However even for those with land to spare, it can be interesting and exciting to keep a few pots and planters perhaps for vegetables that they could consider 'exotic' or just a new vegetable that they are experimenting with.

Whatever the reasons behind growing veggies in pots and containers, the fact is that it can be very rewarding in many ways – and not just nutritional or financial.

It is well known by medical professional's world-over that gardening in any form can have major therapeutic benefits, something that is to be highly valued especially in the hectic stress-ridden lifestyles that so many people find themselves in.

I trust that you have found this admittedly brief work on container gardening beneficial, and I would like to thank you personally for your purchase – it is much appreciated.

Container gardening is a fun and easy way of starting your own garden, especially if you live in an area with little space for gardening. It's an efficient way of doing your part for the environment by planting and recycling materials that can be used as containers for plants.

To enjoy a more effective and productive container gardening, plant vegetables that you can cook and eat. This way, you will be able to save money and enjoy vegetables that are not only fresh or nutritious but of good quality. It is a fulfilling activity that benefits both your physical and mental health. You can also use container gardening to personalize and improve your living area. Plants are very pleasing to the eyes and some vegetables can be used as ornamental plants as well.

Once you've decided to start a container garden, choose the type of vegetables you will plant and the growing medium that you will use. Also, choose a good location and container that is suitable for your plants and available space. Maintain and care for your garden by watering, pruning and fertilizing the plants as needed. Make sure that the plants are able to get the needed nutrients in order for it to produce good quality fruits, leaves and flowers.

Some problems are likely to occur in container gardening. But don't be discouraged; these problems are common even to experienced gardeners. Just remember that these problems can be remedied. To further enjoy container gardening, invite your friends to start their own or ask for some tips from other gardeners living in your area.

Container gardening is very easy and suited even for busy people. So, what are you waiting for, start one now!

Made in the USA
Coppell, TX
20 June 2020